TANK

Breach

TANK

OBERON BOOKS
LONDON

WWW.OBERONBOOKS.COM

First published in 2017 by Oberon Books Ltd
521 Caledonian Road, London N7 9RH
Tel: +44 (0) 20 7607 3637 / Fax: +44 (0) 20 7607 3629
e-mail: info@oberonbooks.com
www.oberonbooks.com

A catalogue record for this book is available from the British
Library.

PB ISBN: 9781786821539
E ISBN: 9781786821546

Cover design by Ellice Stevens

Back cover photograph © The Other Richard

Printed and bound by 4edge Ltd, Essex, UK.

Visit www.oberonbooks.com to read more about all our books
and to buy them. You will also find features, author interviews and
news of any author events, and you can sign up for e-newsletters
so that you're always first to hear about our new releases.

BREACH

Breach is a multimedia performance company founded by theatre-makers Billy Barrett and Ellice Stevens, and video artist Dorothy Allen-Pickard. They collaborate with actors to create politically engaged, formally exploratory shows that blend drama and documentary. Breach's first show, *The Beanfield* – about a 1985 clash between riot police and New Age travelers – was made whilst all three were students at Warwick University, and toured the UK after winning a Total Theatre Award at the 2015 Edinburgh Fringe. The following year, *Tank* was awarded a Fringe First in Edinburgh before its London transfer and Spring tour. Breach is currently developing a third show, *The Drill*, about emergency response exercises and the psychology of rehearsing for disaster.

TANK

DIRECTED BY
Billy Barrett
Ellice Stevens

VIDEO
Dorothy Allen-Pickard

WRITTEN BY
Billy Barrett
Joe Boylan
Craig Hamilton
Ellice Stevens
Victoria Watson

PERFORMED BY
Joe Boylan
Craig Hamilton
Ellice Stevens
Victoria Watson

Bryony Davies performed as Victoria
for various performances due to injury

Commissioned by Battersea Arts Centre with
support from The Bike Shed Theatre, Camden
People's Theatre, Lyric Hammersmith, Moor Theatre
Delicatessen and New Diorama Theatre

THANKS TO

David Byrne, Philip Hansen-Bailey, Shelley Hastings, Colin Henderson, Jack Morning-Newton, Christopher Riley, Isobel Rogers and Sam Wightman

PERFORMANCE DATES

New Diorama Theatre: 28th July 2016
Moor Theatre Delicatessen: 30th-31st July 2016
The Pleasance, Edinburgh Festival Fringe: 7th-20th August 2016
New Diorama Theatre: 6th-10th September 2016
The ShowRoom Chichester: 9th February 2017
Theatre Royal Plymouth: 21st-25th February 2017
Battersea Arts Centre: 13th March-1st April 2017
West Yorkshire Playhouse: 3rd April 2017
The Bike Shed Theatre, Exeter: 4th-15th April 2017
Belfast MAC: 20th-21st April 2017
The Wardrobe Theatre, Bristol: 27th-29th April 2017
HOME, Manchester: 4th-6th May 2017
Birmingham Repertory Theatre: 23rd-25th May 2017
Arts at the Old Fire Station, Oxford: 26th May 2017

Supported using public funding by
ARTS COUNCIL
LOTTERY FUNDED **ENGLAND**

Notes on the Text

In 2015 we attempted a thirty-year anniversary re-enactment of the Battle of the Beanfield, a brutal standoff between riot cops and New Age travelers near Stonehenge. *Tank*, our second show, continues this investigation into the possibilities of reworking history through performance – this time taking cues not from the heritage industry, but the movies.

This show is the product of a year and a half's conversation, improvisation and writing around the Dolphin House experiments of the 1960s – thinking about how they've been represented, and what they might represent. We were alert throughout to how the human-dolphin war of words might act as a metaphor (or an actual example) of the United States' desire for dominion over culture and language during the Cold War – as well as, more urgently, the ways in which fears of the foreign and the unknown are being provoked and exploited today on both sides of the Atlantic.

As such, the words and opinions in this text should not be taken directly as those of the people that inspired them – nor of the actors speaking them. For personal accounts from Margaret Lovatt and her surviving colleagues, a gripping overview of the Communication Research Institute's activities can be found in Christopher Riley's documentary *The Girl Who Talked to Dolphins* – as well as in John Lilly's book *The Mind of the Dolphin*, which includes Lovatt's own detailed diaries of her time with Peter.

Our production of *Tank* is staged as a trippy amalgamation of film pitch, table-read, radio play and rehearsal room. The set consists of a standing office water-cooler, a table with a laptop and two microphones (one distorted, one unaltered) and four chairs. The actors speak to each other and to the audience, using the microphones and following printed transcripts for the verbatim sections – in which Margaret is voiced by **Victoria**, John by **Craig**, Peter by **Joe** and Pam by **Ellice**, each attempting to match extant recordings as closely as possible. The performers slip between roles and accents, as on a screen behind them fragments of film shot in a swimming pool intermittently flicker. Parts of the show have a somewhat improvisational quality, so what's written here is sometimes an approximation of how dialogue tends to play out.

The stage directions provided here are intended to give a useful sense of this, but anyone interested in re-approaching the text of this book with their own vision is invited to do so however they can imagine.

Photograph: Murdo MacLeod for *The Guardian*

[A Cowboy's Work is Never Done – Sonny and Cher
In Dreams – Roy Orbison
Big Iron – Marty Robbins
Navajo Joe – Ennio Morricone]

Onscreen: The rippling surface of an empty
swimming pool.

ONE

The cast enter individually, and each fill a plastic cup from
the water-cooler as the voiceover plays.

Onscreen: The words "John C. Lilly, The Mind of the
Dolphin (1967)".

> **JOHN (VOICEOVER):** The human species has
> found quite empirically that the best
> communication is between those who
> closely resemble one another, placed in
> long-term close contact.
>
> Isolated communities develop and
> maintain singularities in the language
> used; they develop and maintain
> customs of dress, of ritual, of loving, and
> of working uniquely theirs.
>
> They can also develop what has
> been termed "fear of the stranger" or
> "xenophobia". The projection of one's
> fears outward onto the unknown or

the unfamiliar creates a dangerous communication paralysis. In the modern world, with its bombs and threats of extinction, we must carefully examine our best means of communication from group to ever larger group.

We can no longer allow the glass walls that have risen between us to exist.

CRAIG: Somewhere in the Stanford University Special Collections, there are hundreds of boxes of quarter-inch tapes.

ELLICE: They're archived by date, but falling apart.

JOE: To listen to these tapes, you have to bake them at a low temperature for one to eight hours. This is to dry out the moisture that's built up in their binder.

VICTORIA: After several months, they deteriorate and become unplayable.

ELLICE: There's over five years' worth of recordings in this section. Some of these tapes – a tiny fraction – have been baked, played and transcribed.

JOHN: April 1963 – the 65th limited language experiment. The time is 09:36

hours. Sissy, give me the pipe. Pam, give me the ring. Thank you.

VICTORIA: These transcripts are from the Communication Research Institute on the US Virgin Island of St Thomas.

JOE: A NASA funded experiment. Its aim: to teach dolphins how to speak English.

ELLICE: What you're hearing is a verbatim performance of these transcripts.

JOE: It's 1963, and as the world's two superpowers battle for hearts and minds, and proxy wars rage in distant countries, the Kennedy administration focuses its efforts towards space.

CRAIG: John Lilly is the founder of the research centre. He's developing a model for interspecies communication, with the hope that NASA be the first to discover intelligent life.

JOE: And of course, it is vital that this intelligent life learn English before any other language.

CRAIG: John works with dolphins because they are highly intelligent, but also – and this is crucial – they have pre-historic brains. Alien, in a way. The mind of the dolphin is an uncharted territory.

ELLICE: John also knows that dolphins can imitate human sounds through their blowholes. So say you or I were to go "hello", then a dolphin could maybe go…

All take a sip of water and gargle:

ALL: "Heeelllooooo."

ELLICE: Just like that.

> JOHN: Pam give me the brush. Thank you. Pipe Sissy… The time is 10:55 hours. Bye bye, Sissy. Bye Bye.

ELLICE: But the tapes also tell another story.

JOE: The story of a special relationship, which maybe some of you already know.

ELLICE: The relationship between a college dropout, Margaret, and her dolphin test subject, Peter.

CRAIG: *(Indicating VICTORIA and himself.)* We'll be doing – or at the very least trying – American accents, because this is an American story.

JOE: *(Indicating ELLICE and himself.)* And we are going to be modulating our voices using sound software on this laptop.

CRAIG: And we also have this rubber dolphin head…

VICTORIA: We should explain.

ELLICE: The tapes tell a story, but it's only a part of a story.

JOE: We only have fragments. Just glimpses. The tapes tell facts –

ELLICE: But we're filling in the gaps. Piecing it together.

CRAIG: We should start with Margaret's arrival at the institute, Dolphin Point Lab as it was known, on the island of St Thomas.

[Bang Bang – Betty Chung]

TWO

The cast assemble into a line in front of the audience. This is broken occasionally as moments of the action are fleshed out.

CRAIG: April, 1963. And if it were a movie, it would look like this:

JOE: A car, driving along a winding coastal road.

ELLICE: It's red, vintage.

VICTORIA: No, it's turquoise and chrome. Like Greased Lightnin'.

CRAIG: It's battered. The windows are down and –

JOE: And well, it doesn't have a roof –

CRAIG: Yeah.

JOE: So it's roofless and we can see the woman, Margaret, driving.

ELLICE: Silk scarf blowing in the wind behind her.

JOE: And blazing out of the car radio –

VICTORIA: The Beach Boys.

CRAIG: It's Lenny Kravitz, *Are You Gonna Go My Way*.

JOE: It's 1963. It's that Japanese song from *Inherent Vice*.

[Sukiyaki – Kyu Sakamato]

CRAIG: And the engine roars as the car, and it's a red Corvette obviously, swerves around the corner.

ELLICE: She's a college dropout so we're looking at a Volkswagen beetle.

JOE: Margaret: young, obviously. Attractive, sure. She's feminine –

VICTORIA: But rugged.

JOE: Ruggedly feminine. Intrepid.

ELLICE: She's fresh-faced. Sunglasses and long dark hair and she's humming along with the words.

VICTORIA hums along.

JOE: A white building comes into view. Straight white lines, cut into the cliff. Waves actually *lapping* at the edges.

VICTORIA: James Bond would be proud.

ELLICE: Because it is *stunning*. Breath-taking. Like instantly knocks-you-off-your-feet stuff.

7

CRAIG: And then the car would pull into this long gravel drive.

ELLICE: It would crunch underneath the wheels.

VICTORIA: And there's like palm trees and they're like, wafting in the breeze. Hot. Bright. Sunny. Blue skies.

CRAIG: The car door opens and these two long slender legs just, like, swing out.

ELLICE: Right. But we don't excessively linger on these legs.

VICTORIA: Definitely not. Or pan up them.

ELLICE: Yeah, nobody's panning up anything.

CRAIG: I know that, but we notice them.

JOE: Of course, we notice them. Who wouldn't?

–

VICTORIA: And Margaret, she's full of expectation.

ELLICE: Right, *anticipation*, because –

VICTORIA: Because she's at the start of this new adventure at a New Frontier. And she's… a pioneer.

ELLICE: A pioneer!

JOE: Yes.

ELLICE: I love that.

CRAIG: That's perfect. The car door slams shut –

[Sukiyaki cuts out]

VICTORIA: And Margaret, she takes long swinging strides up the drive. Her heels sinking into the gravel.

ELLICE: Not heels, impractical, she's wearing sturdy flats.

JOE: Boots. Made for walking.

ELLICE: Okay, and that's just what they do – and she pushes through a set of doors. There's a secretary at a desk, who's talking on the phone. She looks up like –

JOE: Margaret shouldn't be here. But she smiles.

CRAIG: A pioneer, remember. And the secretary would have said something like "One moment please *ma'am* – yes? Can I help you?"

JOE: And now Margaret would say this one killer line that sums up her whole devil-may-care, no guts no glory, gun-slinger –

ELLICE: Take-life-by-the-balls.

CRAIG: Right, schtick. She says –

VICTORIA: "I heard you have dolphins."

–

CRAIG: And the secretary would nod, repeat: "Yes ma'am. *Can I help you?*"

ELLICE: But Margaret's undeterred.

VICTORIA: She wants what she came for.

ELLICE: Because she's *hungry* for it.

JOHN: 66th limited language experiment on the 8th April 1963. The time is 13:41 hours. First session with polyethylene line attached to objects.

ELLICE: John Lilly. In the middle of a language lesson with two dolphins.

JOHN: Pam – attach me the line. Sissy, give me the brush… Thank you! Pam – give me the pipe. Thank you!

JOE: His secretary calls to him over the tannoy. Somebody's here to see him.

JOHN: 14:00 hours – end of session. Bye bye!

VICTORIA: His white lab coat swings out behind him as he walks through those narrow corridors.

CRAIG: We hear beeps and clicks. And another science noise.

JOE: He pushes open a big door and when he appears, she smiles.

VICTORIA: A grin. Pearly whites.

ELLICE: She's got great teeth.

CRAIG: And the next thing, Margaret would've run towards him and thrown her arms around him.

JOE: No, she barely bats an eyelid.

ELLICE: Well, she shakes his hand.

VICTORIA: "I've heard so much about this place – it's great to finally meet you!"

ELLICE: See, John Lilly, he's about to invite Margaret, this stranger, to join him at the institute so she's going to have a certain professionalism about her.

JOE: So, shaking his hand she would say –

ELLICE: Professional.

VICTORIA: "John Lilly? Margaret Howe. I heard you have dolphins! And I'd like to talk to you about *those* dolphins."

JOE: As they talk she'll recount how her brother-in-law told her about some dolphin house in St Thomas over dinner, and how she just could not stop thinking about it ever since.

VICTORIA: At the first opportunity, she jumped in her car –

JOE: The black mustang.

VICTORIA: To come and find out more.

ELLICE: And John appreciates her confidence.

VICTORIA: Her courage.

CRAIG: It's her pizzazz.

JOE: They walk back out into the sun, onto the balcony, where down below some dolphins are swimming in a pool.

CRAIG: And there are three dolphins. Just glistening –

JOE: Little shiny black eyes –

VICTORIA: Alien –

CRAIG: Diving down –

JOE: Little white teeth –

CRAIG: Splashing around –

JOE: Gun-metal grey skin –

ELLICE: And the dolphins all have their own unique traits and John is introducing them. So there's Peter, Sissy and Pam.

CRAIG: John would have said something like: "Have you seen the movie *Flipper*?"

VICTORIA: "Sure I have."

CRAIG: "Pam used to be a movie star. Do you see that scar down her side? She got speared in some kind of stunt. That's Peter, he came here from another research facility."

JOE: And Margaret feels a particularly affinity with Peter, because, well –

VICTORIA: "That one! He seems to have this – confidence, a curiosity about him, doesn't he?"

ELLICE: And Margaret sees something of herself in him here, because we know that she's never studied biology, or linguistics, or actually anything else at all relevant here.

CRAIG: *But* her confidence, her natural fascination for the animals, her desire to broaden her horizons, these things would make her a top-rate researcher so –

JOE: So, John obviously infers this as well, because he gives her a pen and paper and asks her to observe the dolphins' behaviour.

ELLICE: And Margaret notices straight away that the dolphins seem to combine sound and movement in order to talk to each other.

CRAIG: "Yes, dolphin communication is sort of *embodied*, different combinations of movements with sound mean different things."

VICTORIA: And Margaret says, straight up, "Can you speak dolphin?"

ELLICE: John pauses. Maybe laughs a little.

CRAIG: "No – no – I'm gonna make those dolphins speak English."

[Bang Bang – Betty Chung]

THREE

JOE and VICTORIA are seated at the table facing one another behind their microphones, reading from printed transcripts. ELLICE and CRAIG are separate, downstage.

MARGARET: 1, 2, 3, 4 – this is the yellow mic. 1, 2, 3, 4 this is the orange mic. Okay.

Hello Petey. Hello. Back up. Back up. Today is July 22nd, I'm with Peter, AM lesson. Hello.

PETER: Hello.

MARGARET: Clearly, Peter. Again, let's say, "Hello".

PETER: *Blows bubbles.*

ELLICE: July, 1964.

CRAIG: It's morning.

ELLICE: So – the sun. We can almost feel it on our skin.

CRAIG: Almost hear the breeze rustling through the trees as Margaret – now a researcher at the centre – sets up a series of microphones.

ELLICE: She dangles her legs in the cool water.

MARGARET: Peter. Oh! You. Do you know what this is? Say ball! Peter. Ball.

PETER: *Clicks.*

MARGARET: English.

CRAIG: She lifts a ball out of the water.

ELLICE: Yep, holds it up – like this.

CRAIG: More like this.

ELLICE: And she says –

MARGARET: Ball. Ball.

PETER: *Whistles.*

ELLICE: Her mouth opening wide and slowly. She's exaggerating the movements of her lips –

CRAIG: Pulling out every possible sound from the word.

ELLICE: Yeah, and later, Margaret actually starts to paint her face white and she wears black lipstick, like some sort of mime artist, to really draw his attention to her mouth, you know. To make her mouth look like his blowhole.

MARGARET: Hmmmmmm. Again Peter. Say. Ball.

PETER: *Clicks.*

MARGARET: Start in English Peter. Ball. Ball.

PETER: *Tries.*

MARGARET: That's better yes! Now you are getting there! Simple things Peter. Come on!

ELLICE: And it sounds like she needs to be the one in control here, like –

CRAIG: She's this cowboy.

ELLICE: Exactly, and Peter's this wild stallion.

CRAIG: She has to ride him hard.

ELLICE: Break him in.

MARGARET: Now let's go back. Listen. Ball.

PETER: *Tries.*

MARGARET: No!

PETER: *Tries.*

MARGARET: Ball.

PETER: *Tries.*

MARGARET: No! Ball. Ball. Ball.

PETER: *Tries.*

CRAIG: She throws the ball to the far side of the pool.

ELLICE: Pronunciation and comprehension. That's what she's looking for here. She wants him to say the word "ball" back to her, and then fetch it when asked – show he understands what "ball" actually is.

MARGARET: Say it clearly Peter. Come on. You are alright. You are doing well. Proud of you! Ball!

PETER: *Tries.*

MARGARET: Try again. Listen. Ball. Listen. Ball.

PETER: *Tries.*

MARGARET: Yep. That's it! No more Peter. Good. Counting Peter. Counting. 1,2.

PETER: *Bubbles.*

CRAIG: And when Peter does follow these orders – when he gets them right for the first time – we can hear Margaret's elation.

ELLICE: Pride. Like a mother watching her child take its first steps.

MARGARET: That's better. English Peter. 1, 2, 3, 4.

PETER: *Squeaks.*

MARGARET: No. Peter begin with 1.

PETER: *Joins in with Margaret's 1, 2, 3, 4.*

MARGARET: 1, 2, 3, 4. That's better.

ELLICE: And the lessons, they're –

MARGARET: Let's do it all again.

ELLICE: – very repetitive.

MARGARET: 1, 2, 3, 4.

PETER: *Whines.* (continues)

MARGARET: Keep it up Peter. 1, 2, 3, 4. This one is called 1, 2, 3, 4. Hello.

PETER: *Clicks.* (continues)

MARGARET: NO! NO! Hello.

PETER: *Clicks.*

MARGARET: NO! Wrong Peter. Try some
more.

PETER: *Tries 'Hello'.*

MARGARET: Yes. That's better. Come right
out with the English Peter. Don't even
think in your own language. English, all
the time!

[Bang Bang – Betty Chung, played in reverse]

FOUR

All are gathered around the table. CRAIG is seated behind his microphone, JOE stood on his chair. ELLICE and VICTORIA face the other two.

JOE: So now there's a jump forward in the tapes.

JOHN: Tape Number 5 at four minutes of six on January 19th 1965.

ELLICE: Inside.

VICTORIA: A corridor.

JOE: Margaret, wearing a lab coat, creeping towards an open door.

VICTORIA: She edges forwards.

ELLICE: Closer now.

JOE: Towards the sounds of humming electrics, splashing water.

VICTORIA: Makes it to the door and – steps through?

ELLICE: No, she freezes. Waits on the threshold.

JOHN: Peter on two CC's of LSD.

VICTORIA: Okay, and looks in.

JOE: At the laboratory. Between the machinery, Margaret can see John's arm, holding up a glass bottle.

ELLICE: In his other hand, he has a syringe. She watches as he sticks the needle into the top of the bottle, which is full of a clear liquid.

JOE: Her palms sweat.

VICTORIA: She holds her breath.

ELLICE: She's sceptical.

VICTORIA: Uneasy.

JOE: Of course she's uneasy, because what does he think is actually going to happen here? What's this going to achieve exactly?

VICTORIA: But she's still the amateur.

ELLICE: Still, after two years, Margaret is the newcomer. She wants to take Peter out of this, but she can't. So she says nothing, can't stop Lilly from pulling up the plunger.

VICTORIA: From carrying the big glass syringe over to Peter. Her heart's beating out of her chest.

JOHN: Peter is throwing the ball outside the tank. I'll put it back in.

ELLICE: And he's saying something fatherly now, just like, "be a big boy …"

PETER: *Deep breaths.* (continues)

CRAIG: Try to relax. Take a nice deep breath in, and on the outbreath now you're going to really relax, let go of all that tension. Well done, really good. You're doing really well. And in a second now, you might feel a little prick. Just a scratch. You might not even feel it. And 3, 2, 1.

ELLICE: He stabs the needle into Peter's exposed side.

VICTORIA: And Margaret sees – or perhaps only thinks she sees – Peter's eyes slam shut. Hears a splash as he thrashes. A scream, a fury. She can hardly stand to watch.

Onscreen: Close up of JOE's eyes, red with chlorine, blinking rapidly.

[Nothing's Going to Hurt You Baby – Cigarettes After Sex]

JOHN: 10.06 PM, tape number 8… is it? Peter and LSD 200 microgram dose continued. This is about the beginning of the 8th hour.

VICTORIA breaks into a slow, sensuous dance like a classic Hollywood star. Gradually ELLICE, JOE and CRAIG join her in a choreographed routine blending 1960's dance crazes like the twist with swimming motions and Western shootout tableaux. The music slows and distorts as the cast break from their dance.

FIVE

VICTORIA: John – John – John –

Beep.

JOE: Margaret, helmet on, makes the long walk to the capsule to get back in touch with ground control Major John.

VICTORIA: *(As astronaut.)* John? John? Come in, John? Can you hear me, John?

Beep.

ELLICE: She's got curlers in her hair, pom poms in her hand and just this idea that's going to like rock his world.

VICTORIA: *(As cheerleader.)* John, I was like looking at the dolphins today and I was like wouldn't it be cool if we took one of them and put it in a room and I was there too and I was like its mother and stuff?

Beep.

JOE: Not one to fall back, she wants boots on the ground and choppers in the air.

VICTORIA: *(As soldier.)* Let me lay out my offensive for Operation Rolling Ocean Blizzard Storm.

Beep.

CRAIG: February 1965.

CRAIG and VICTORIA face one another, downstage.
ELLICE and JOE watch from the water-cooler.

VICTORIA: *(As MARGARET.)* John, this is going to
sound *crazy*, but I was watching this TV show
last night – this family show where the mother,
she was cooking dinner, and everything was
burning and going wrong. Because her baby
was crying and she kept having to run back to
it, and then check on the chicken, and then go
back to the baby, and –

CRAIG: He has three beads of sweat on his
forehead. She has this tick. A nervous tick,
where she taps the tip of her middle finger
against her thumb while she speaks.

VICTORIA: It made me think we might be going
about all this the wrong way. We're building
minds here. We should be structuring our
lessons like a mother teaches a child. I've been
thinking about when we leave the lab at night
– when we all get in our cars and, you know,
we pull down the garage doors and we just
drive on away and go back to our families, and
our homes and – I've been thinking – what if
we didn't all leave? What if we didn't just leave
these big brains floating around on their own
for twelve hours at a time? What if we lived

with the dolphins? Full time, no distractions. Here. Had the opportunity to stay with them around the clock? John, I want to plaster everything and fill this place with water.

CRAIG: He raises a hand to silence her – and she is silenced because it's the 60s and that's the social context.

JOE: A pause.

CRAIG: He nods.

ELLICE: He likes it.

JOE: He lays out the routines she'll follow –

VICTORIA: No, she plans everything.

JOE: Okay – so, for ten weeks Margaret will live with Peter.

CRAIG: She will teach him in this new model of learning, the way a mother teaches a child. And she will live with him in isolation.

VICTORIA: And she's about to do something unprecedented for the time here. She's a trailblazer.

SIX

ELLICE and VICTORIA are seated at the table facing one another behind their microphones, reading from printed transcripts. JOE and CRAIG are separate, downstage – as in Three. During this section, they seem occasionally to be squaring off like cowboys in a Western.

CRAIG: She is. But before we get there, we need to know a few things first. So, March, 1965. A preliminary experiment in which Margaret and Pam live together for seven days, seven nights, to work out the ideal conditions for dolphin-human cohabitation.

MARGARET: I am a good girl.

CRAIG: An upstairs room of the laboratory. Pam is in a tank in the middle of the room.

JOE: There's a bed hanging by four ropes, a TV on a shelf, a desk.

MARGARET: I am a good girl.

PAM: *Whines.*

MARGARET: I must eat my fish.

PAM: *Whines.*

MARGARET: I must speak for fish.

PAM: I eat my fish.

MARGARET: It's very soft but it is humanoid.

CRAIG: Margaret observes Pam as she lays in sixteen inches of water.

MARGARET: I learn to speak. I learn to speak.

PAM: *Gurgles the syllables.*

MARGARET: Yes…yes! I speak English.

PAM: *Gurgles.*

MARGARET: I speak English… English. English.

PAM: *Clicks.*

MARGARET: Speak English. Speak English. Okay. Learn to speak. Learn to speak. Learn to Speak. Okay Pam.

PAM: *Gurgles.*

MARGARET: *(Laughing.)* You are so clever and so pretty. It's okay… It's okay.

CRAIG: Pam's back is breaching the surface of the water. Sixteen inches just doesn't even cover her. Her back has been dry for so long that the tissue is cracked.

JOE: Bleeding.

CRAIG: Sure. This is actually probably quite traumatic. But Margaret presses on.

MARGARET: Speak for food! Speeeeeak! Speak. Hello!

PAM: *Tries.*

MARGARET: Yes Pam! Now we speak. Okay! Good girl. I like to eat!

PAM: *Screeches.*

MARGARET: Alright. Hello. Hello. Thank you. Thank you!

PAM: Thank you.

JOE: The blood is congealing now like a can of red paint spilt in the sun, baked into a solid sheet. Right there. The blood begins to drip down her sides into the tank, with all the piss and shit, the rotting uneaten fish around her. You see, the upstairs tank, *(American accent)* it don't have no filtration system in it yet, so all that filth and decay gets into her eyes, up her nose, down her throat.

CRAIG: Down her – Sorry, I don't think there's blood.

JOE: No?

CRAIG: No, I think Margaret notices the back is sore, but there's no blood. She's not a monster.

JOE: Okay, nobody's calling her a monster. She cares about Pam. So she pushes water over, trying to keep it wet.

CRAIG: Realises the water actually needs to be a bit deeper.

JOE: Sixteen inches. Whilst perfect for a human –

CRAIG: For a dolphin, not so much.

MARGARET: 1…2…

PAM: *Tries.*

MARGARET: 1, 2, 3.

PAM: *Clicks.*

MARGARET: 1, 2, 3, 4.

PAM: *Clicks 3 syllables.*

MARGARET: Try again, Pam.

JOE: She will decide on twenty-two inches next time and a 6ft deep swimming area.

CRAIG: A space where the dolphin can be a dolphin – because, as Margaret says herself, "although we don't have to respect their privacy, we should respect their happiness."

MARGARET: 1, 2, 3, 4, 5.

PAM: *Clicks 5 syllables.*

MARGARET: Oh, you are such a good girl. Alright. I'm going to end here.

SEVEN

[Quicksand – Martha and the Vandellas]

JOE: With the experiment with Pam deemed a
success... Four months later.

JOHN: 1965 Method of establishing
close contact, chronically, with
Turciops Truncatas, for interspecies
communication research. Use of the
mother-child teaching model: Human
"mother' and young male dolphin.
John C Lilly and Margaret C Howe,
communication research institute,
dolphin point lab, St Thomas, US Virgin
Islands.

*During this section, a floorplan of the upstairs
laboratory is mapped out with masking tape
stretched across the backs of the four chairs, pushed
into the corners of the stage. Black tape from the
inside of VHS tapes is strewn across the floor, where
it merges with a growing pile of plastic cups.*

JOE: The top floor of the house. Furniture moved.
Wallpaper stripped. Thick white plaster pasted
onto walls. A hose, coming in through a
window, filling an office thigh-high with water.
This process, the filling, the plastering, happens
three times until there are no more leaks.
Hanging by hooks from the ceiling: A bed, a

shower, a stove. John Lilly is walking around the room, plugging in microphones – one in each corner, some underwater.

Onscreen: VICTORIA ties up her hair and puts on a diving mask.

VICTORIA: I put on a black swimming costume hanging on the bathroom mirror. Pull it up my legs, up my body and put my arms through the holes.

I pick up a pair of scissors by the taps on the sink. I grab my long hair in one hand and cut it off. I walk into the room filled with water. Feel it as it moves between my legs. I walk onto the balcony and look out as Peter is coaxed onto the sealift. He's rising and rising in the air.

I watch as he just hangs in the sky. This otherworldly creature. I watch as he's taken up by the lift, into the flooded lab above. Our new home.

"Good boy, good boy, good boy…"

EIGHT

[Lay in a Shimmer – Pantha Du Prince]

JOE and VICTORIA are penned into the taped-out square like boxers in a ring, whilst ELLICE and CRAIG are able to move freely in and out of it as they watch the action unfold and direct the other two.

JOE and VICTORIA take the microphones from their stands, and circle one another slowly. VICTORIA reads from her file of printed transcripts, but JOE does not. During this section, these two performers gradually become less distinguishable from their characters.

ELLICE: June – August 1965.

CRAIG: This is it, what it's all been building towards. Margaret and Peter living together.

MARGARET: Eat the fish please. Eat the fish please. Speak for fish. Good fish. This is a fish. This is a fish. I see Peter fish. Speak for fish Peter. I see Peter fish.

PETER: *Wails.*

MARGARET: Peter eat fish. Peter eat fish.

PETER: *Makes a loud splash.*

Onscreen: JOE and VICTORIA slowly swim towards each other underwater.

MARGARET: No Peter. Squirt. Squirt. Squirt.
Squirt. Speak for fish. Don't squirt! Don't
squirt. Speak. Speak. Speak Peter. Peter
eats fish.

ELLICE: Week one. The first few nights are awful.
You are uncomfortable and you can hardly
sleep. Now you've made the water deeper you
find it difficult to even walk across the flooded
room. It's like wading through concrete.

CRAIG: It's difficult adjusting to everything being
wet all the time.

ELLICE: Like your bra hooks, they've warped in
the water and scratch your back constantly,
like nails.

CRAIG: And Peter is always around, following you
underfoot. She can't go anywhere without you
getting in her way – you are like a petulant
toddler holding on to her ankles.

ELLICE: She has to carry around a broom to bash
you away.

PETER: *Whines.*

MARGARET: *Imitates Peter.*

I'll be back Peter. I'll end here. Think about it
Peter.

CRAIG: When you're not stalking her round the tank, you spend a lot of time talking to yourself in the mirror.

ELLICE: Week two. Maybe you're screaming to get out?

CRAIG: We don't know that he's screaming. Are you screaming? I don't think you're screaming.

ELLICE: But, maybe you *are* screaming. Maybe you think she's trapped you here against your will. Because you start to get violent.

CRAIG: Of course you do. You're just letting off steam.

ELLICE: You find your way between Margaret's legs and push them apart.

CRAIG: And you shout when he hurts you. Week three.

ELLICE AND CRAIG: / Come on baby.

Onscreen: JOE and VICTORIA circle one another underwater.

MARGARET: Come on baby. July 23 – Noon lesson with Peter. I've just been playing with him and he's a bit snappy!

ELLICE: You're finding your new home too small.

MARGARET: Hello. Listen. Hello! Can you say Margaret?

PETER: *Tries.*

MARGARET: Let's do it again. Margaret.

PETER: Margaret.

MARGARET: Gooooood! Good Petey. Listen. Listen. Say Ball.

PETER: Ball. *Screeches.*

MARGARET: Christ you bit me.

Onscreen: JOE and VICTORIA speak to each other underwater, air-bubbles erupting silently from their mouths.

ELLICE: Week four. You can't exercise as much. Whenever you try to move across the room, Margaret's always in your way. It's *her* treading on top of *you.*

CRAIG: But the yelling and aggression is fleeting. You get closer. A companionship begins to form.

ELLICE: Okay, that's interesting. So maybe, you take your lunch every day in the flooded room. And you sit at the desk, and it quickly becomes a habit but you don't remember when you start doing it – you just throw a bit of whatever you're eating to him.

CRAIG: A pop tart.

ELLICE: Not a pop tart; it's a spoonful of jello.

CRAIG: It's definitely a pop tart. Week five. You make progress – You learn that by rolling onto your side, blowhole slightly out of the water, this produces a great "m" sound. That is progress.

ELLICE: Progress or not though you're becoming increasingly aggressive.

CRAIG: You knock her down.

ELLICE: He's playing a game.

CRAIG: But you're making her bleed.

ELLICE: I mean, it's not a human game – he doesn't understand that.

CRAIG: You don't realise that she gets hurt. Until he understands that none of this will be comfortable for you.

MARGARET: He seems very unhappy. Or are you just fed up Pete?

ELLICE: And Margaret, she starts feeling increasingly isolated.

Onscreen: Shot from below, JOE and VICTORIA tread water. He pushes her underwater and holds her there for a second. She bobs back up.

CRAIG: Yeah, you're always in this room, always wet –

ELLICE: You aren't sleeping because Peter, frustrated, splashes you throughout the night.

CRAIG: You drape a shower curtain around your bed so that it stays dry.

ELLICE: For sleep, or privacy – it doesn't matter. Peter throws the ball against the curtain – it wakes you up.

CRAIG: In your boredom you've taken to repetitive acts of play.

ELLICE: Week six. You've picked up a monotonous whining tone.

CRAIG: You yell at him to stop it. Week seven.

ELLICE: If he makes a noise that isn't humanoid, you decide you won't even look at him to see what's wrong, what's going on, what he's trying to say. It's like you don't care. Why don't you care?

VICTORIA: I do care.

Onscreen: JOE drags VICTORIA around underwater, who thrashes to try and escape his grip. He pulls out her arm and opens his mouth to bite it.

CRAIG: That's interesting because I don't think you care when he makes those sounds. I think you're bored. See, Peter is constantly looking for attention but you can't always give it.

ELLICE: Don't feel bad, I mean he's a dolphin. And he's getting too rough to handle.

CRAIG: He's trying to engage. But it's on a dolphin level. Isn't it, mate?

MARGARET: Okay. Peter. Come on. Hi. Kisses. Come on Peter. Come on. Now. Come on Peter. Kiss Peter. Kiss.

PETER: *Kissing noises.*

MARGARET: Did you say kiss? Come on.

Onscreen: Shaky camera movements as JOE and VICTORIA violently struggle with one another underwater – it is unclear who is in control as they push, pull and writhe around each other's bodies.

PETER: *Clicks.*

MARGARET: Peter come on. Say those kisses.

PETER: *Tries.*

MARGARET: You are heavy, Peter.

ELLICE: You are vicious, Peter. As an adolescent dolphin, estimated to be between five and six years old, you've started to get erections numerous times a day. And when you do you're so aggressive in your arousal you knock her down with a flick of your tail.

CRAIG: You're an animal. You're used to having sex eight times a day. And it's this rambunctiousness you find most disruptive.

Onscreen: JOE playfully performs backflips and barrel rolls underwater for VICTORIA as she counts with her fingers: 1, 2, 3.

MARGARET: Okay. Kiss – Hi.

PETER: *Clicks.*

MARGARET: Kiss. Kiss. Speak Peter. Speak. Come on.

PETER: *Clicks.*

MARGARET: Okay. Say it again. Say it again.

NINE

[Lay in a Shimmer fades out]

JOE remains still, blank, throughout as the others watch him intensely.

ELLICE: I just get this real sense that you're trying to get the words. You know, when you're not distracted, or throwing yourself against the walls, or yelling at yourself in the mirror or overtaken by these unsatisfied sexual urges, I think you're *really* trying. Are you? Are you trying? What do you think Margaret? Don't look at me, look at him. Looking at him right there, what do you think he's thinking about? Is it the words?

VICTORIA: I don't know.

CRAIG: Okay.

VICTORIA: I think – maybe he wants – I think he wants to swim over to me.

ELLICE: And what does he want?

VICTORIA: He wants to swim over to me and start nuzzling my legs.

ELLICE: Gently?

43

VICTORIA: Yeah, gently at first but then his teeth will start to come out.

ELLICE: Hurting you a bit.

VICTORIA: Yeah he wants to hurt me.

CRAIG: Then he wants to hold your head underwater.

ELLICE: Playing?

VICTORIA: Yeah playing at first. So he'll let me get up.

CRAIG: He'll let you stand up again.

VICTORIA: Then he'll just push me right back over.

ELLICE: Okay.

VICTORIA: He'll hold my head down for ten seconds. Then as I get up, he wants to swim over and press his fin –

ELLICE: Sure.

VICTORIA: Then he wants to keep pressing the fin so that it's cutting me open. So that he's using his fin as a knife.

ELLICE: Right. And would that – I mean, would that even work?

VICTORIA: No.

ELLICE: No.

VICTORIA: But he wouldn't care.

CRAIG: Okay.

VICTORIA: He'd want it to break me open – he'd want it to rip through my internal organs. He wants to break through my organs so that he's destroying my whole body.

ELLICE: Just getting right in there.

VICTORIA: He wants to break me like that until – well until I'm dead basically.

CRAIG: Okay.

VICTORIA: Then he wants to grab my body with his teeth, and bash it against the walls of the tank.

ELLICE: Okay, so the white walls?

VICTORIA: Yes, he wants to make the white walls red, and make sure I'm dead. Then he wants to drag my body out of the tank and onto the beach.

ELLICE: Interesting. So what we'd have would be blood on sand.

VICTORIA: And he'd want to probably stick a flag pole through my desecrated corpse.

CRAIG: Sorry, and is that through your stomach or your lungs?

VICTORIA: My bloody stomach.

CRAIG: Good choice.

VICTORIA: And he'd probably want to be filming it.

ELLICE: Okay, and is he filming this on a smartphone?

VICTORIA: Yes – or, well no. He wants news cameras to be there.

CRAIG: Okay so you're on national television, with a flag pole stuck through your, well I suppose at this point it must be your cadaver really.

VICTORIA: Yes, and then he'd probably want to get a barrel of petrol.

ELLICE: So in your mind, this is about to become a burning?

VICTORIA: Exactly. So then, I think he wants to pour the petrol over my body, and just set fire to it –

CRAIG: Sorry, could we also make it a stoning as well?

VICTORIA: Yeah, we can do that.

CRAIG: Great.

VICTORIA: So he wants to pour petrol over me, set fire to me, and then thousands of dolphins would come out of the sea, and walk up the beach.

CRAIG: Walk?

VICTORIA: Sorry, yes, they've learned how to walk on their tails –

ELLICE: Okay, that's clever.

VICTORIA: And there's so many of them, dolphins upon dolphins upon dolphins.

CRAIG: Man dolphins, woman dolphins, children dolphins, and they would all have a stone.

ELLICE: So presumably they've taken these stones from the ocean?

VICTORIA: Exactly, held between their fins.

ELLICE: Clever.

CRAIG: So let me picture this. You're on fire.
   On the beach. And you can see the flames
   reflected in Peter's eyes as he looks down the
   camera, and you're surrounded by all these
   hordes of dolphins, all with a stone. And
   they're ready to throw –

VICTORIA: Yes.

ELLICE: And how does that make you feel?

   –

VICTORIA: Well, I imagine I don't feel anything
   because –

ELLICE: Because sorry, you'd be dead already.

VICTORIA: But if wasn't I'd probably be thinking,
   you know, what could I have done?

   –

ELLICE: So interesting.

TEN

[Orca – Anna Meredith]

CRAIG: Margaret begins to understand Peter's struggles with the lessons. And, although her fear never truly subsides, during week eight Peter softens. Tries a different tact.

ELLICE: He stops drawing blood. He modifies his advances to a more human, civilised level.

CRAIG: Now, when aroused he's quite gentle. She's not bruised every night. Peter is courting her.

ELLICE: And Margaret realises she needs to do something. Week nine. She can hardly stand to watch anymore and she reaches a point where she needs to do something about her fear, about Peter's aggression. And she can't keep sending Peter back down to the sea pool, so he can – 'engage' with Pam and Sissy – you know, it's exhausting. For both of them. Margaret feeling like she's going backwards in the lessons. And Peter, going up and down, up and down in the elevator constantly. So Margaret needs to find a way to help Peter out.

CRAIG: Yeah, and she does this by just wanking off his massive, great big dolphin cock.

ELLICE: No that's not what it is.

CRAIG: It is what happened though.

ELLICE: No – what she does – it made sense. She was feeding him, teaching him, *living with* him. This didn't seem like that far of a stretch. It was about what was best for the lessons. For both of them. It wasn't a big deal. So it was when Peter learnt to manoeuvre into a different position, one where he could gently slide between her legs and present his, his *penis* so it was easily rubbable by a hand or a foot – that she – did it.

CRAIG: And Peter accepted either, didn't he? He's certainly not fussy. This happened three times before the lessons even started.

[I Really Love You – The Tomangoes]

Onscreen: JOE climbs out of the pool and makes his way to the changing room, where he sits on a bench and slowly eats an entire mackerel.

JOE puts on the rubber dolphin mask, and VICTORIA covers the lower half of her face in white makeup and applies black lipstick – as described in Three. They dance in unison – a looser, more aggressive dance than previously, but repeating a few of the same movements. The pace intensifies until VICTORIA struggles to keep up with JOE and she watches as he collapses on the floor. She pulls off his mask.

MARGARET: Oh right! It's all gone Peter. He absolutely astounds me. I think he's wonderful! Peter you are delightful – you are a pleasure to work with, Peter. He listens. He hushes. He tries so hard. I'm very pleased with him. I think you are wonderful Peter. Here's your toy fish.

ELEVEN

Throughout this section, CRAIG and ELLICE watch from outside the floorplan as JOE and VICTORIA interact slowly, physically, animalistically: opening their mouths as wide as they can, crawling on the floor on their knuckles like apes, VICTORIA attempting to bear JOE's weight as he loses the ability to stand upright.

CRAIG: So on one level then, it's this love story.

ELLICE: Is that what we're saying?

CRAIG: It's what we've been saying, yes.

ELLICE: I don't remember ever having *explicitly* agreed on that.

CRAIG: Okay, but on one level, clearly it's this odd couple love story, about a woman and this, this *Other*, overcoming difference together.

ELLICE: Like co-existence?

CRAIG: Exactly.

> *Onscreen: VICTORIA, shot from below, treads water. JOE emerges and circles her, before pulling her down to the bottom of the pool.*

ELLICE: Right, but it's just that it's not *only* that, is it?

CRAIG: I mean I think it goes without saying that Peter is in love with Margaret, Margaret is in love with Peter.

ELLICE: Because of the…

CRAIG: The sexual stuff, yes.

ELLICE: Okay – I don't really know where to start with that. I think there's maybe a lot of assumptions that are connected with the – you know, the prurient – the masturbation issue.

CRAIG: Because that's the best bit.

ELLICE: Okay. But are you aware that animals get masturbated in captivity like all the time?

CRAIG: You're going to have to explain that one.

ELLICE: Will do, for example: you take a farmer who masturbates a bull to inseminate a cow, right? He will manually stimulate that bull until it ejaculates into a tube. That tube will then be quickly frozen in liquid nitrogen and it will stay there for maybe six months, five years. And then six months or five years later, another farmer will remove that tube from the thermos flask. He will empty its contents into a long metal syringe. He will lead a cow out into a field. He will lift up her tail. He will stick his hand *directly* into her rectum. There he will grab hold of her cervix. He will then stick the needle through the cervix, so it reaches her uterus, where he will depress the plunger and deposit the contents. Now, by anyone's logic, are either of those farmers in love with either the cow or the bull?

CRAIG: Probably not.

ELLICE: No, probably not. Because what the farmers are doing has a purpose. Ultimately to produce livestock to sell, so we can eat it.

CRAIG: And here, she masturbates the dolphin because he has these energies.

ELLICE: These aggressive energies which are causing him to be disruptive. She needs to help him use them up so that they can be productive again.

CRAIG: Make progress.

ELLICE: It's not an *expression* of anything. And besides that, it's public. People can watch.

CRAIG: People can watch, but it's sensual. She's said herself that it was "sensual".

ELLICE: True. But she also said "mechanical". A biological function.

CRAIG: Okay, well if Peter didn't love Margaret, then why does he kill himself when he's taken away from her, and moved to Miami?

ELLICE: No, no that's not what happened.

CRAIG: He did! He committed suicide.

ELLICE: Okay, yes – you're right. Peter did commit suicide. Because dolphins *can* commit suicide, but it was nothing to do with Margaret. Peter killed himself two years after the ten-week experiment and it was because he was moved to this awful laboratory in Miami where he couldn't move, wasn't fed properly, was effectively shitting into his own mouth. He didn't kill himself because of heartbreak – he just looked around and knew he was fucked. And I know you, and I know what I'm like, and I think if either of us went from getting fed constantly, stroked all the time, told we're good, wanked off three times a day before we even had to get out of bed in the morning and then were put into a dark, grimy tank where we were being ignored and starved, I think we might just do the same thing.

–

CRAIG: Okay, fair point. But presumably, this looks like love. A little?

ELLICE: Maybe.

CRAIG: And to Peter, to the dolphin, it *feels* like love.

ELLICE: Okay, fine. So, it looks like love and to the dolphin it feels like love. Fine. But underneath that, we need to be clear that something else is happening.

CRAIG: Right, sure. The progress.

ELLICE: No, it's not that. She's *destroying* something. She's not listening to him, to what's already there – it's not her fault but –

CRAIG: Well *he's* listening. He's learning. More and more every day. Getting better and better.

ELLICE: At speaking?

CRAIG: It's more repeating.

ELLICE: That's the whole thing. Margaret can say "ball, ball, ball" as many times as she likes, and Peter might eventually make a noise that sounds close to "ball", but that doesn't mean he *means* ball.

CRAIG: Okay, but even if he's not getting the language, he's getting something.

ELLICE: So, what does he get?

CRAIG: Fish.

–

ELLICE: Sure, he gets the fish.

CRAIG: He likes the fish.

ELLICE: Needs the fish.

CRAIG: Needs it. Grateful for it.

ELLICE and CRAIG exit.

TWELVE

Onscreen: Blue.

JOE and VICTORIA face each other, by this point exhausted.

MARGARET: I'm feeding Peter upstairs.

I did not eat last night.

VICTORIA: And now it's over. The experiment, the ten weeks. Finished.

JOE: Yeah, there's no fanfare. No love-conquers-all. No "you'll never take me alive". That's it. It just ends.

VICTORIA: We leave the top floor of the lab.

JOE: You go back to your office, me to the sea pool.

VICTORIA: And the room is drained. All that water. Gone.

JOE: I think they turned it back into an office or an archive – you know, paperwork stuff.

VICTORIA: I still work at the lab, everyday, with you and the other dolphins.

JOE: With Sissy and Pam. And I won't touch you again.

VICTORIA: The lessons continue for another two years – just as before.

JOE: But your grand idea of immersing me in English, in your cultures and customs… Well, it didn't really work. I just didn't make the kind of progress you were hoping for.

VICTORIA: I'm defiant though. To this day, I maintain that had I been given more time with you, I'd have made a real breakthrough.

JOE: But really though, I didn't make any progress. Not in the ten weeks, not the whole five years. I challenge you to listen to those tapes, and see if I make any improvement. My oration, it's basically the same in 1967 as it is in '63. You have to really search for anything, even a few seconds, that sounds just a little bit like human speech. Most of the time, it's just noise.

VICTORIA: And NASA agrees, because in 1967 they pull funding for Lilly's research and Dolphin Point lab is forced to close. But, I stay there. I stay living in the dolphin house. I get married.

JOE: To who?

VICTORIA: John Lovatt – the photographer who documented the experiment. And I raise my children in the upstairs room.

JOE: Teach them how to speak?

VICTORIA: Yeah.

MARGARET: I did not eat last night.

I will eat all my fish.

JOE: But the institute –

VICTORIA: It's shut down. The dolphins are placed into individual glass tanks and lowered into a truck.

JOE: A truck, driving along a winding coastal road.

VICTORIA: What colour is the truck?

JOE: I don't know. And blazing out of the stereo, it's –

VICTORIA: Nothing. Just noise. And there's scenery. Deserts. Greenery. Mountains. It's difficult to make anything out, everything is out of focus. We see the day turn to night, turn to night, turn to night.

JOE: A sign: "Welcome to Miami"…

The sound of static and feedback.

Onscreen: Cut between closeup of VICTORIA's mouth speaking and JOE's eyes watching, with increasing speed.

JOE: And it's dark	MARGARET: Please give
It's, er, Chlorine	me my fish.
It's Ball	
Ball. Ball. Ball	
Small	I will speak for my fish.
Small tank	
Closed up	
Close up	I will speak for my fish.
Up up up	
A Science noise	I must speak for fish.
Salt	
Pipe	
Pipe	I can speak for my fish.
Point Blank	
blank Tape	
Tap	
Tap "That's a wrap"	I did not eat last night.
Wrap	
Rattle	
Rattlesnake	
"There's a snake in my boots"	I did not eat last night.
But. Cigarette butt	
Bat	
Hat	
10 gallon. Smith and western	I did not -
Worsen	
Hearsen	
Hearse	
High	I am hungry.
High noon	
My moon	
Boom box	

Blare   I am hungry.

Blood. Blood box

Flood. Flood box

10 paces

Space   Speak when I speak.

Race rocket

Fuel

Pump

Action   Speak when I speak.

Movie

Star

Star   Say what I say.

Star

Star

You're a star. You're a star. You're

a star. You're a star!

                                         Say what I say.

[Gyöngyhajú lány – Omega]

*JOE begins to retch, splutter and cough, whilst VICTORIA
keeps speaking her transcript. As the music builds,
CRAIG returns dressed as a cowboy. VICTORIA attempts to
calm JOE and keep his eyes on her as they both feel CRAIG
approaching and see him raise his gun, pointed at JOE.*

*ELLICE enters. In one hand she has a plastic cup full of
fake blood, and in the other a blood-pack. She hands
JOE the cup and bursts the blood-pack on his chest. He
sips from the cup, then touches his chest and, noticing the
blood on his fingers, spits out more. He raises his arms*

and falls in slow motion, like the ending of the Vietnam War film Platoon – his mouth open in a silent scream.

Black out.